GOD AND US

GOD

and

US

by Benedict J. Groeschel, O.F.M., Cap.

ST. PAUL EDITIONS

NIHIL OBSTAT:
    Rev. Richard V. Lawlor, S.J.

IMPRIMATUR:
    ✠ Humberto Cardinal Medeiros
    Archbishop of Boston

    The transcripts of Father Benedict's six one-half hour television lectures were sponsored by the Diocese of Portland, Maine.
    Special acknowledgment is given to the editor of the television series: Clarence F. McKay, Director, Communications Office of the Diocese of Portland.

ISBN 0-8198-3029-1 cloth
        0-8198-3030-5 paper

PHOTO CREDITS
J. D. Tifper—cover
Dore—14
Sahata—27
L. Hernandez—29
Fra Angelico—31, 75
A. Mari—61
E. Giaroli—73 top

Printed in the U.S.A., by the Daughters of St. Paul
50 St. Paul's Ave., Boston, MA 02130

The Daughters of St. Paul are an international congregation of religious women serving the Church with the communications media.

To the Most Rev. Edward C. O'Leary
Bishop of Portland, Maine
who made the series possible

c.1

CONTENTS

Creation and Being 15

The Incarnation 30

Passion and Resurrection 43

The Holy Spirit.............................. 54

The Church 62

The Forgiveness of Sin,
  The Resurrection of the Body
  and Life Everlasting 76

The Reverend Benedict J. Groeschel, O.F.M. Cap., is the Director of the Office for Spiritual Development of the Archdiocese of New York. He is also the Director of Trinity Retreat, a center for prayer and study for the clergy.

Father Benedict was Chaplain of The Children's Village in Dobbs Ferry, New York, for fourteen years until assuming this post for the Archdiocese.

Father Benedict obtained his Master's in Pastoral Counseling at Iona College in 1965 and his Doctorate in Psychology from Colombia University in 1971 and teaches Pastoral Psychology at Iona, Fordham, Saint Joseph's Seminary and Maryknoll. He also directs St. Francis House, a residence for homeless young men in Brooklyn.

In June, 1979, Father Benedict co-authored a work on St. Catherine of Genoa in *The Classics of Western Spirituality,* published by Paulist Press. He has also published a number of articles on pastoral counseling and spiritual direction.

Creation and Being

We live in an unbelieving age. It is a time when many people who once believed, are no longer sure they believe anymore; when many things, especially in media and frequently on television, undermine the foundations of belief. I would like to ask you to join with me for the next six programs as we take a look at faith and belief. We are going to use as our outline the very simple prayer which most Christians learned by heart years ago, The Apostles' Creed.

"I believe in God, the Father Almighty, Creator of heaven and earth". This is the first article of the Creed and we will spend some time in meditation on what it means to believe in God. Perhaps you who watch this program are not a believer, you have often wondered about people who do believe. Perhaps you are some-one who grew up in a family of people who did believe but you do not. Perhaps you do believe, but you do not understand the meaning of the mysteries you believe. My interpretation, although based on the teaching of the Catholic Church, should be largely consistent with the faith all Christians believe. Today's program on creation should be of equal importance to Jewish and Moslem friends who are watching the tele-vision as well as those others who are seeking for God.

Let us start with the first stupendous statement. I **believe in God**.

We have to begin with something that everyone agrees on and that is the material world. It is something that we all experience. If you walk around your house and put your hands on various objects, or look out the window, see the sky and, perhaps, the trees in the field, you are part of an immensely complex system. Events that take place thousands and even hundreds of millions of miles away from where you live, affect your life and sustain it, or can terminate it. If you look down into a microscope, you will see a world of infinitely small detail which makes it possible for your body to continue to function. And if you look up into the sky, you see around you objects which are trillions of trillions of miles away. In fact, beyond the planets and the sun, the nearest object to us is a star called Alpha Centori. It is our closest neighbor and it is 4½ light years away, which means it is 4½ times six trillion miles away.

In the night sky, there are bright objects which are as much as 11 hundred light years away, which means they are eleven hundred times six trillion miles away. There are distant objects, which can be faintly seen, which are totally outside of our star city or galaxy. These objects, like the Andromeda Nebula, which can be faintly seen with the human eye and easily seen with binoculars, are more than a million light years away.

Where did it all come from? To that question there are several answers which we should look at. It had

been the assumption of most scientists in the last 200 years that the world was always there. Science assumed that whatever the building blocks of the material world were, they were eternal. They had neither beginning nor end; and although the shape of the universe would change, although it would pulse into life and then fall back into nothingness, there were always present the basic building blocks. The atoms of this universe were everlasting. In a certain sense this view absolutely denied the statement of the Creed, **I believe in God, the Father Almighty**. Frequently science in its prejudices has been deeply atheistic.

A great many people have found such a view of scientists totally incomprehensible. First of all the universe operated with too much order and design; physical laws were absolutely predictable, and out of the swirling gases of this primeval soup had come an extraordinarily beautiful and complex world. Now we have seen the other planets as the space crafts make their mysterious way around these other worlds — worlds of beauty and order and design, although frequently filled with the turbulence of life unfolding. There is the immense complexity of the earth, with its systems of life — vegetable, animal and human. All this, along with the unbelievable complexity of a single human life, cause many people to believe that indeed the world is guided by a mind, by reason. The easiest thing to assume is that this mind or reason is something like a world's soul · that is, something unified with the world and yet something beyond all things in a mysterious way.

Dr. Robert Jastrow, professor of physics at Columbia University and director of the Goddard Institute of NYSA, has provided us with a remarkable book called **GOD AND THE ASTRONOMERS**. I would like to quote a passage from the remarkable conclusions of Dr. Jastrow . . .

"Science has proven that the Universe exploded into being at a certain moment. It asks, What cause produced this effect? Who or what put the matter and energy into the Universe? Was the Universe created out of nothing, or was it gathered together out of pre-existing materials? And science cannot answer these questions, because, according to the astronomers in the first moments of its existence, the Universe was compressed to an extraordinary degree, and consumed by the heat of a fire beyond human imagination. The shock of that instant must have destroyed every particle of evidence that could have yielded a clue to the cause of the great explosion. An entire world, rich in structure and history, may have existed before our Universe appeared; but if it did, science cannot tell what kind of world it was. A sound explanation may exist for the explosive birth of our Universe; but if it does, science cannot find out what the explanation is. The scientists' pursuit of the past ends in the moment of creation. This is an exceedingly strange development, unexpected by all but the theologians. They have always accepted the word of the Bible; In the beginning God created heaven and earth. To which St. Augustine added, "Who can understand this mystery or explain it to others?" It is unexpected because science has had such extraordinary success in tracing the chain of cause and effect backward in time. We have been able to connect the appearance of man on this planet to the crossing of the threshold of life, the manufacture of the chemical ingredients of life within stars that have long since expired, the formation of those stars out of the primal mists, and the expansion and cooling of the parent cloud of gases out of the cosmic fireball.

Now we would like to pursue that inquiry farther back in time, but the barrier to further progress seems insurmountable. It is not a matter of another year, another decade of work, another measurement, or another theory; at this moment it seems as though science will never be able to raise the curtain on the mystery of creation. For the scientist who has lived by his faith in the power of reason, the story ends like a bad dream. He has scaled the mountains of ignorance, he is about to conquer the highest peak; as he pulls himself over the final rock, he is greeted by a band of theologians who have been sitting there for centuries."

This quotation is very startling, because it suggests the reversal of the original scientific prejudice against creation. It was so startling that as Jastrow points out, Einstein himself was reluctant to admit this conclusion because it would bring him to the notion of creation. Fr. Lemaître, a Belgian priest and astronomer, cajoled Einstein into accepting the conclusion called the "big bang" theory of creation.

This world soul might be called the god of the naturalist. The philosopher, Benedict Spinoza had this idea of God. Albert Einstein, the great modern scientist, said that he could accept the notion of Spinoza's god. However, if there is such a god, and we might best call that kind of god a world soul, it is not a creator. It is the creation itself. This god would be co-extensive with the material world and would be exactly the same age as the world, and it would unfold with the world.

Perhaps, even you thinking yourself to be a Christian, believe in a world soul. This belief is contrary to Christianity, Judaism and Islamism, which among the religions of the world most loudly proclaim that there is a single mind which has created the world out of nothing, which stands beyond the world and which knows the world. In the case of most Jews, Christians, and Moslems this mind is believed in some way to know that which it has created and to care for this creation. We believe that there is indeed a Creator. Modern man likes to be his own master, lord, god and judge. Therefore, the idea of belief in and surrender to a mysterious, unknowable Being, who knows us, thus giving up some of our tendency toward curiosity and the urge to know all things — this idea of belief challenges very many of the assumptions of modern society. Yet this is what the Apostles' Creed proclaims, **"I believe in God, the Father Almighty, Creator of heaven and earth"**. Following the Book of Genesis, Christianity maintains that the Bible gives not so much a literal scientific description of the beginning of the world but a magnificent symbolic summary of incomprehensible events. Christianity believes that God, as a single All Powerful Being, in a single instant, called out of absolute nothingness a material world, and guided it on its way. The beautiful description in Genesis, coming from an ancient people, who originally composed it without the use of written materials or even written language, carefully goes through stages of creation from the beginning of light to the appearance of man. Yet the stages in Genesis present an outline that startlingly follows any scientific description of the beginning of the universe as we know it.

In the early 1930's the scientific community was shaken by a growing realization that the world indeed was not eternal. Much of the realization resulted from the discovery by Albert Einstein of the theory of relativity. The theory of relativity brought scientists to the conclusion that all of the atoms in the universe were the same age. You know that there are a tremendous number of atoms in a lead pencil. All of the atoms in the whole universe, from galaxy to galaxy of this unbelievably immense cosmos in which we live, all of these atoms are exactly the same age. They began in the same instant, in a fiery explosion setting the universe on its unbelievably long road which finally led to the existence of man, who as far as we know, is the only being in that whole cosmos who can look up to the stars and know that they are there — the only one who can question his own existence.

This is the misuse of creation because of the failure to recognize God. The only other position is to believe, to reach up beyond what you are. For me it is to reach up beyond my own selfish and personal narrow set of limits. We need to look out and recognize responsibility for all of creation and especially for the human creation. If you are a believer, let me ask you this — Do you act as if creation is God's gift to us? Do you take care of it? Do you receive it as a precious thing? Do we protest in any way against the ruin of creation by chemical pollution and by environmental destruction? Do we cry out at all against the contemporary destruction of human life in a vast number of ways? Do we believe that life is precious? Do we care for human beings? Do we see that animals are delivered from torture and unnecessary pain? Do we watch out for children; do we abuse the poor; do we misuse creation?

Fortunately, modern human beings are beginning to face themselves with these questions. With the little bit of creation that God has given you, how do you protect it, care for it, cherish it, love it? Do you see God in creation; do you pause to see Him in the glory of the sky, the magnificence of nature? Do you see the tragedy of evil in children led into delinquency and sin? Are you concerned about people who starve? Do you give of your own substance to see that the things of creation are more equally distributed? In a word, do you care? Do I care? To come to any realization of a Creator is to bring into our own heart the idea that Dr. Jastrow suggests, that after we look at the entire world, we must see it is guided by a knowing mind. If you do this you are then approaching belief. It goes beyond demonstration. There is no other answer, but this answer must be accepted by belief. Belief is a gift which the Creator gives to the creature so that He can be known. God created human beings to be free, to have some spark of the divine fire, to be able to say yes or no to Him, for all of the rest of creation serves Him with an absolute determination which is irresistible. The whole of the world is bound to reflect the glory of God, except human beings. Human beings can bring glory to God and peace to themselves, or they can bring blasphemy, hatred and self destruction. Do you believe? One does not come to believe by simply willing to believe. It is not the matter of a persuasive argument. As Cardinal Newman said, "Even to be convinced is not to be persuaded, because belief is God's gift." Faith is when God reaches out to you and to me and we reach back.

In our next program we will move on to the belief in Christ as the Son of God. It is Christ who revealed that the Creator was also our Father who loves and cherishes and seeks all of His children to share His life with them. It is Christ who calls us to see our provident Father in the lilies of the field, and the birds of the air. It is Christ's great apostle Paul who in the Letter to the Romans reminds us that Creation shows forth the power and divinity of God for all to see, and it is Paul who focuses our attention on the emphatic teaching of Christ that we are the children of God.

Let us assume, for the moment, that Jastrow and the other scientists are reluctantly correct, that everything in the universe began in a single moment. Let us assume that it has been guided in mysterious ways to the creation of human beings, to the little child who wants not to die; to the old person who ponders about life, and asks what it means; to the young person who idealistically does good; to the wicked person who turns away from the goodness of creation and imposes upon others his own idea that he is God, as we see was done by the Nazis in the Second World War. Consider all of these people, and their responses to creation; those who seek to do good with it, those who seek to maintain it selfishly for themselves and those who corrupt it, and you begin to approach the mystery of belief. The prophets of Israel and the saints of the Church all proclaim together, **I believe in God, the Father Almighty, Creator of heaven and earth**. They agree that in all of this, there is a loving, caring mind to whom we can relate as our gentle Father; that this entire universe is made by Someone who knows us.

Today you must ask yourself what your response to such a Being is. If you do not believe, then you must ask yourself the question of God. What would the world be like if no one believed? If there was no question of God? What would it be like if human beings forgot the word God, or the idea of creation? We would then become a world of highly skilled animals. There would be kindly and benign animals and there would be vicious animals, but all would forget to wonder if the discrete incidents of life had any meaning at all. All the events of life would be random, one happening after another, without rhyme or reason. Nothing would hold the universe together and nothing would hold the individual person together.

By chance I went to see a picture of this world recently. Someone suggested that I go to see a movie, and it turned out to be a movie in which people did not believe in God; a young man drawn on to suicide, his parents each desperately looking for meaning in their lives. They were good people but people for whom life had no meaning. That is true atheism. There are people like the people in this movie who thought that God was just a world soul, which can be placated by some kind of magic, sometimes by a superstitious use of Ouija boards and the like. Others believe the much greater superstitions which come from the misuse of science, that science will always have the answer. There are those who think that science will always give meaning, even though the abuse of science at this very moment in our history threatens us with total destruction. Recently in the **New York Times**, there was an article about a meeting of scientists which took place not very long ago. They calmly decided that if a 50 megaton nuclear bomb exploded in the air over New York City, it would kill 2 million people instantly and 7 million people would die in the course of two weeks. They also concluded that it was highly probable that such an event would happen, and that there would be a nuclear war. And they went on to point out that if all of the nuclear weapons in the world went off at the same time, the earth would be obliterated as a center of life for all.

Perhaps no figure in Christian history brings together this teaching of the Prophets, of Christ and of St. Paul better than does St. Francis. To St. Francis, God is the gentle Father of Creation and Christ our loving Saviour and brother. Shortly before the end of his life in 1225, St. Francis composed the Canticle or Hymn to the Sun. May I ask you to join with me in meditation on the Canticle of the Sun.

Most High, all powerful, good Lord
to you all praise, glory and honor and all blessing;
to you alone, Most High, they belong.
and no man is worthy of naming you.
Praised be you, my Lord, with all your creatures
especially for Brother Sun
who brings day, and by whom you enlighten us;
he is beautiful, he shines with great splendor,
of you, Most High, he is the symbol.
Praised be you, my lord, for Sister Moon and
    Stars;

in the heavens you formed them, clear, precious,
and beautiful.
Praised be you, my lord, for Brother Wind and for
the air and for the clouds,
for all seasons by which you give life to your
creatures.
Praised be you, my lord, for Sister Water, who is
very useful
and humble, precious and chaste.
Praised be you, my lord, for Brother Fire, by
whom you enlighten
the night, he is beautiful and joyous and strong.
Praise be you, my lord,
for Sister our mother the Earth,
who nourishes us and bears us,
and produces all kinds of fruits,
with the speckled flowers and the herbs.
All praise be yours, my lord, for those who grant
pardon
for love of you, through those who bear trials and
weakness,
happy are they if they endure in peace; by you,
Most High they will be crowned.
Praise be you, my lord, for our Sister bodily
death, from whom no
living man can escape. Woe to those who die in
mortal sin!
Happy are those whom she shall find in your holy
will,
for the second death can do them no harm.
Praise and bless my Lord
and give him thanks, and serve him with great
humility.

(Translation: Fr. Regis Armstrong, O.F.M. Cap.)

The Incarnation

"I believe in Jesus Christ, His only son, Our Lord, who was conceived by the Holy Spirit and born of the Virgin Mary."

These words which we have said all of our lives sum up an event which is as stupendous in its proportions as is the first creation of the world. You will recall that in our last program we began with the astronomical theory called "the big bang". That means that all the matter in creation, all the particles of matter, began to exist in exactly the same moment of time. The size, the depth, the awesomeness of creation pass before our eyes. And yet the second creation of the world, the spiritual creation in Christ, of which we speak today is more awesome in that it is a creation which will last forever. The material world which began so startlingly and unthinkably with a single explosion will pass away with all of its variety and splendor. The spiritual creation which began so silently and in quiet shall not pass away.

The spiritual creation of the world means that the Son of God came into the world to enable human beings to become the adopted children of God. The second creation of the world can be summed up in a single word, the name of a single person, **CHRIST**. And it is to the mystery of the Incarnation that I call your attention. In this meditation and in our next one we will look into some aspects of the immense mystery of Christ.

I must confess to you that there is nothing I would rather speak about than the mystery of Christ. In very dark moments of my own life, sometimes in years of darkness, it was only Christ who was with me to save me. Those who have not had an experience of Christ in their whole life find it difficult to understand this. I must say that anyone looking at world history and at the impact of the life of Jesus Christ who was born and lived and died in obscurity must pause and wonder, who is He? What was He like? But it is only the person who has had the experience of Christ who can understand in some way what this mystery is.

A contemporary example of the mystery of someone coming to know Christ is provided by Archbishop Anthony Bloom, a very popular spiritual writer who is also the Metropolitan Archbishop of the Russian Orthodox Church in Western Europe. Archbishop Bloom in his book, **Beginning to Pray** (Paulist Press) tells us how he as a young displaced person growing up in Europe, was very hostile to religion and especially to Christianity. He was invited to a lecture by a Russian priest and he disliked the lecture. "I became more and more indignant, I saw a vision of Christ and Christianity and that was profoundly repulsive to me. When the lecture was over I hurried home in order to check the truth of what the priest had been saying. I asked my mother if she had a book of the Gospel because I wanted to know whether the Gospel would support the monstrous impression that I derived from his talk. I expected nothing good from my reading so I counted the chapters of the four Gospels to be sure I read the shortest, not to waste time unnecessarily. I started to read St. Mark's Gospel. While I was reading the beginning of St. Mark's Gospel, before I reached the third chapter, I suddenly became aware that on the other side of my desk there was a presence, and the certainty was so strong that it was Christ standing there, that it has never left me. This was the real turning point in my life. Because Christ was alive and I had been in his presence, I could say with certainty that what the Gospel said about the Crucifixion of the Prophet of Galilee was true and what the centurion said was right when he said, 'truly he is the Son of God'. It was in the light of the resurrection I could begin to read with certainty the story of the Gospel, knowing that everything was true in it, because the impossible event of the resurrection was to me more certain than any event in history."

Great numbers of people, of many different Christian denominations, have had this experience of Christ. So even the curious who have not had it must stop and ask themselves sometime, what do I think of Jesus Christ? The mystery of Jesus Christ begins with the fall of man. If we look at the marvel of creation and the beauty of the material world, and the human being as the absolute known pinnacle of that creation, the creature that is capable of knowing what the stars are, and then we look at human history, we realize that there is something desperately wrong. We see that human beings are not only the most creative of all living things, but they are the most destructive. The different religions of the world refer to this in various ways as the fall of man. The question has arisen seriously in the minds of many men as to how an individual is to be saved, or perhaps how was the world to be saved. How can the human race find its way out of the dark tunnel into which it has entered?

I do not have time on this program to ponder the mystery of evil as deeply as I might. As someone who has worked all his life with poor people, let me tell you that the mystery of evil is visited on the poor with ferocity and disdain every day — on poor children, on old people, on the physically and mentally ill. They are the principal victims of evil.

Among those who sought their way out of the problem of evil in the ancient world were the Gnostics. They believed that within the human being there were qualities that were like God. If one cultivated these qualities, one would become less and less a being of this world where evil was such a strong component, and one would become more and more a being of the world of the spirit. Thus a human being, by the knowledge of the divine, would come to be divine-like and would survive the most terrible of evils which they saw to be death. The answer to death, to oblivion, to the absolute destruction of the human being, could be found by becoming god like.

It was from the Jews that a different message came. The Jewish people understood, by reason of the teaching of the prophets, that human beings could only be saved if they were part of the people of God, and if they became loyal followers of God's law. Salvation was available to the Jew if he followed Moses and the prophets. It was available to the devout Gentile if he followed the law of nature. Salvation was given only by God. It was God's gift. It was often unclear in the long centuries of Jewish history whether this salvation was individual or if it was in some collective way a salvation. Some thought it was the earthly establishment of the kingdom, some thought it was a kingdom beyond the grave, and some thought it was both. Nevertheless the prophets kept summoning Israel to the belief in a Messiah, that someone would come who would be the holy one of God, the Saviour.

Indeed it is the belief of Christianity that in a very dark moment of human history, a calm before the breaking of a terrible storm, in the humblest of ways, God came to be with His children. God came to dwell among human beings.

It is important to note that in this advent, the coming ultimately depended on the free will and acceptance of a human being. Salvation would be God's gift, but it had to be accepted. It had been lost by the first parents of the human race, mysteriously described in the events of the Book of Genesis, and it would be recovered by the free consent of the human being who would accept the absolute salvation of God.

It is fruitful to meditate on the fact that this event took place in the most silent of ways. Just as no one had ever heard the explosion that was the "big bang", just as no one hears the cosmic events in the sky because they go on in a world where there are no ears to hear them, so also the event that would be the recreation of the world took place in the absolute silence of the inner being of a single human.

I am going to read the words of Sacred Scripture, the Gospel of St. Luke, describing this event which is the second creation of the world. It is as mysterious and spellbinding, as utterly overpowering to the human intellect as the great explosion at the beginning of creation. But this time it includes the freedom of the human will. The human will had once chosen evil, now it would choose good. In the First Chapter of Luke's Gospel we read these words, "In the sixth month the Angel Gabriel was sent by God to a town of Galilee called Nazareth, to a virgin betrothed to a man named Joseph, of the House of David; and the virgin's name was Mary. He went in and said to her, 'Rejoice so highly favored! The Lord is with you.' She was deeply disturbed by these words and asked herself what this greeting could mean, but the angel said to her 'Mary, do not be afraid; for you have won God's favor. Listen! You are to conceive and bear a son, and you must name him Jesus. He will be great and he will be called, Son of the Most High. The Lord God will give him the throne of his ancestor, David; he will rule over the House of Jacob forever, and his reign will have no end.' Mary said to the angel, 'But how can this come about, since I am a virgin?' (the angel answered) 'The Holy Spirit will come upon you and the power of the Most High will cover you, and the child to be born will be holy and called Son of God.' "

This is an utterly mysterious event. Theologians suggest to us that we do not try to understand all aspects of this event. Take what is obvious, what a simple person can understand; a messenger of God (that is what an angel means) comes to a young girl. She is frightened, as any devout Jew would be in the presence of the signs of Almighty God, and yet she consents. She responds with her **yes**. "Behold the handmaid of the Lord". And thus the second creation begins with the consent of a human being. Many people are confused or puzzled by the devotion of Catholics and Orthodox Christians to the Virgin Mary, but this event points out the absolutely key position that she held in the mystery of the coming of Christ.

I have been in Nazareth. I have been to a spot where there is a sign that says, "In this place the Word became flesh". You can never forget what that young girl did when you kneel in Nazareth.

It is difficult for many people to even begin to comprehend what the meaning of the mystery of Christ is. It means exactly what Christianity has said it meant since the beginning and in utterly mysterious ways. Following the words of the first revelation of the conception of Christ, the Catholic Church has taught that a being who was Divine became at the same time human. The Church teaches this within the context of monotheism (the belief that there is only one God). It took the Church 300 years of persecution to be able to cope with this mystery in words, and it presented its belief in what is known as the mystery of the Trinity. We see that mystery beginning to be revealed in the words of the Gospel of St. Luke where the Most High, the Son of the Most High, and the Holy Spirit are spoken of at the beginning of the history of salvation. The fathers of the Church would struggle for a total of 450 years about how to state this mystery in terms that brought it into full focus. They would finally say, that the child of Mary was a true human being, who had a human mother, but that it was an utterly mysterious being in that He was both human and divine. Divinity was not superimposed on humanity nor did it destroy humanity. Christ was completely human and completely divine. Do not expect to understand this any more than you would expect to understand the "big bang".

Let me put it into our modern frame of reference. According to the teaching of the Church, if Jesus Christ was born today, He would be just like the rest of us. He would get a social security card, He would be counted. If He became a carpenter He would have to join a union. As a little boy, His mother would have to take Him to get His shots. He would have to learn his ABC's. And yet burning down within the heart of this little child, would be a divine nature, something utterly different from what you and I have. This little child would grow up to be a man who would say, "Before Abraham came to be, I am". His disciples and His apostles would come to believe of Him that he had come down from God and that He had returned to God.

In our next meditation we will consider the mystery of redemption — His death and resurrection and second coming. But pause to just think about the mystery of His life. You must step back, you must be filled with the glory of this presence. St. Francis was so anxious to communicate the meaning of this life to the simplest of people that he instituted the Christmas crib. Allow yourself to kneel with the saints of God before the mystery of the Incarnation. When people come and tell you that Christ cannot be God because if He were God He could not be man, don't listen to them. Listen to the saints. Listen to the fathers of the Church. Listen to the words of the Sacred Scripture itself which are the foundation of what the saints and fathers teach.

There once was a man who hated Jesus Christ. He hated all that He stood for. He tried with every fiber of his zealous being to destroy any remembrance of Christ after His death, he persecuted the disciples of Christ and then one day, he met Jesus Christ and this is what that man would say, "Blessed be God the Father of our Lord Jesus Christ, who has blessed us with all spiritual blessings of heaven in Christ. Before the world was made, he chose us in Christ, to be holy and spotless, and to live through love in his presence, determining that we should become his adopted sons, through Jesus Christ for his own kind purposes, to make us praise the glory of his grace, his free gift to us and his Beloved son in whom through his blood we gain our freedom, the forgiveness of our sins." (Ephesians 1:3-7)

These words of St. Paul, like the experience of Archbishop Bloom, like the words of countless other people in the history of Christianity, record the response of the individual to Christ. In Christ we become the adopted children of God. Our salvation does not depend on anything we come to know as the Gnostics taught, but rather on the fact that we are known by God, that Christ becomes our brother. Jesus Christ in the course of His life identified Himself continuously with the poor, the outcast and the rejected. In His description of His second coming, He says, "I was hungry and you gave me to eat; I was thirsty and you gave me to drink; I was a stranger and you took me in". This is the mystery of Christ. It is God among us. It is Emmanuel.

If you are a disciple of Christ, if you have come to believe, if, to use the phrase so dear to many evan-

gelical Christians, you have made Christ your Saviour (which we surely should do), if you have done this, then I ask you to look at your life and see if it reflects the mystery of Christ. Jesus called His disciples to follow His teaching, "If you love me keep my commandments." Are you growing in your own life in following the teachings of Christ?

I ask you to meditate with me at the end of this program on the favorite prayer of Mother Teresa of Calcutta, and it is a prayer that sums up what the Christian response to Christ must be.

"Dear Jesus, help me to spread Thy fragrance everywhere I go. Flood my soul with Thy spirit and life. Penetrate and possess my whole being so utterly that all my life may only be a radiance of thine. Shine through me, and be so in me that every soul I come in contact with may feel Thy presence in my soul. Let them look up and see no longer me but only Jesus! Stay with me, and then I shall begin to shine as Thou shinest, so to shine as to be a light to others; the light, O Jesus, will be all from Thee; none of it will be mine; it will be Thou shining on others through me. Let me thus praise Thee in the way Thou dost love best by shining on those around me. Let me preach Thee without preaching, not by words but by my example, by the catching force of the sympathetic influence of what I do, the evident fulness of the love my heart bears to Thee. Amen.

Cardinal Newman

Passion and Resurrection

We pause now to look at this most profound sub-ject, summarized so succinctly in the Apostles' Creed, "He suffered under Pontuis Pilate, was crucified, died and was buried. He descended into Hell; the third day He rose again from the dead. He ascended into Heaven and is seated at the right hand of God, the Father Almighty". One is overwhelmed at this mystery of the Creed. Each word is filled with mystery and life. As we look at this stupendous outcome of the mystery of the Incarnation, the second creation of the world, we see the infinity of God's love com-municating itself with force and power. But now we must pause to look at something new, the drama of the relationship of the creator with the free creature. This drama is only seen when we look at the relation-ship of God to free creatures, those who share in His divine freedom, in the ability to determine their own destiny and what they wish to do.

The material cosmos is stupendous, but there is no drama. There are no choices to be made. The stars, the planets, the atoms all move by the absolute iron law of nature. But the human being moves freely. He can do what he will, and that is where the drama comes in. Whenever God has been in relationship with free creatures, as happens in the mysterious world of angels or in the equally mysterious world of human beings, there are dramatic possibilities; to serve or to refuse to serve; to love or to hate; to believe in or to reject God. There are all kinds of possibilities that deeply affect the destiny of the creature; to be a child of God or to be a rebel; that is, to make oneself an enemy of God and to be lost in the futility of that struggle with the infinite. There is always the drama of heaven and hell. Nowhere do we see this drama more clearly acted out than in the life and death of Jesus Christ.

Today, we will look at the mystery of the life and death of Jesus Christ from below, as it were, from His earthly life. In our last conference we paused to look at the heavenly things, the divine nature which Christ as Word brought into the world. Now we look at the un-folding of the drama.

In order to simplify this meditation, we will focus our attention on Christ as teacher, brother, priest and king. Each one of these roles weaves in and out of the Gospel. Each one of them is present all the time, but we can focus on one after the other in order to em-phasize for ourselves the different things that Christ is to us.

May I ask you parenthetically at this moment, to be sure to read one of the Gospels in the next day or two. Many people are not familiar enough with Sacred Scripture. There are many good translations of the Scriptures available. Select one you can read. If you have never done so, sit down and systematically read the Gospel. If you are not that familiar with Scripture, begin with the Gospel of St. Mark. It is wise to read a good commentary and introduction to the New Testament as you read along. In the student's edition of the Jerusalem Bible, there are very good introductory explanations for those who unfortunately are not familiar enough with the Scriptures. Read one Gospel after the other, trying to read a Gospel in its entirety. Then you must read the great commentaries on the Gospel, and the first great commentaries are the Epistles of St. Paul and then the Johannine letters or Epistles of St. John. Other informative commentaries may be bought, but none surpass the commentary on the Gospel which are the lives of the saints and great Christians. To me these are the most authentic of all commentaries because they show how the Gospel can be lived out in human life.

As we pause to think of Christ as Teacher, remember that a person teaches, especially in moral affairs, much more effectively by what he does and is, than by anything he says. The entire life of Jesus Christ is the teaching of One who at every single moment was totally and absolutely dedicated to the reign or wisdom of God. Students of the life of Christ have said that at all times He sought to do the will of the heavenly Father. He even startles us by saying this in a mysterious way, by proclaiming that "I have not come to do my own will, but the will of Him who sent me". If you wish to grow in your spiritual life as a Christian, you must make Christ your first teacher. Every one of the saints of the Church proclaim in different ways what St. Paul summed up so beautifully, "Let this mind be in you which is in Christ, Jesus."

The second role of Jesus Christ, I have called the role of our Brother. And I think that this word emphasizes in the most poignant way that Christ has taken on Himself the universal experience of all human beings, that is, suffering and death. Every human being endures pain. Some endure it well, some endure it badly. It is part of the mystery of the Incarnation that the Son of God never exempted himself from the human condition, that at no time did He call a legion of angels to deliver Him although He said that He could. It was part of the mystery of divine love revealed in the Incarnation that God became man and would without exception drink the cup of human pain and be baptized with the baptism of life. No place is this more clear than in the passion and death of Christ, where He permits himself to be subject to the most banal, wretched, and ruthless of political hacks, to cheap, expeditious people who operate on nothing but the pragmatism of the present moment. He takes the place of countless numbers of people who are condemned and even killed innocently because of political expediency in this world. And those who are responsible for His death are accountable not for the death of the Son of God (because they did not realize He was the Son of God), but rather they are responsible for the death of an innocent man who represents all the innocent human beings who have gone to death because of the selfishness and egotism of others. St. Paul sums it up beautifully in a line, he says, "He who knew no sin, became like us in all things but sin". This is why the saints have always seen the mystery of divine love proclaimed most forcefully in the passion and death of Christ. It is why St. Francis loved Jesus crucified. It is why St. Ignatius

Loyola was deeply moved by the passion of Christ. It is why St. Teresa of Avila and St. John of the Cross founded their whole school of spirituality on the passion and death of the Son of God. Every saint of the Church, every great **Christian** of every Christian denomination and church has had the cross of Jesus Christ imprinted deeply on his or her heart. To understand well that Christ became our brother you must recall that the cross for ancient people was a symbol of death, of capital punishment in the most wretched and ignominious way. By reason of His acceptance of the cross as a complete act of obedience, of subservience as a human being, of a complete taking on of the human condition, Christ transformed this symbol of death into a symbol of life.

This brings us to the third role of Jesus Christ, our Priest. It is the duty of a priest to reconcile men to God by means of a sacrifice. The sacrifice is an act which makes something which is indifferent holy to God. The word in English comes from the Latin **SACRUM FACERE**, that is to make holy. It was the work of Jesus Christ to undo the disobedience of the human race, which is epitomized in the fall of the first parents. It was the work of Jesus Christ to bring back, to restore in a most profoundly loving way, the relationship which was meant to exist between human beings and their Creator. May I quote to you the words of the Vatican Council and the Encyclical of Pope John Paul II, **Redeemer of Man**, on this subject. The Pope writes:

"Rightly, therefore, does the Second Vatican Council teach: 'The truth is that only in the mystery of the Incarnate Word does the mystery of man take on light. For Adam, the first man, was a type of him who was to come, Christ the Lord. Christ, the new Adam, in the very revelation of the mystery of the Father and of His love, fully reveals man to himself and brings to light his most high calling.' He who is the image of the invisible God is Himself the perfect man who has restored in the children of Adam that likeness to God which had been disfigured ever since the first sin. Human nature, by the very fact that it was assumed, not absorbed, in Him, has been raised in us also to a dignity beyond compare. For, by His Incarnation, He, the Son of God, in a certain way united Himself with each man. He worked with human hands, He thought with a human mind. He acted with a human will, and with a human heart He loved. Born of the Virgin Mary, He has truly been made one of us, like to us in all things except sin, He, the Redeemer of man." As we reflect again on this stupendous text from the Council's teaching, we do not forget even for a moment that Jesus Christ, the Son of the living God, became our reconciliation with the Father, He, and He alone, who satisfied the Father's eternal love, that fatherhood, that from the beginning, found expression in creating the world, giving man all the riches of creation and making him "little less than God" in that he was created "in the image, and after the likeness of God." He and He alone also satisfied the fatherhood of God and that love which man in a way rejected by breaking the first covenant and the later covenants that God "again and again offered to man". The redemption of the world - this tremendous mystery of love in which creation is renewed is at its deepest root, the fullness of justice in a human heart - the heart of the first-born Son - in order that it may become justice in the hearts of many human beings, predestined from eternity in the first-born Son to be children of God and called to grace, called to love."

It is in the cross on Calvary, that we see Jesus Christ as the High Priest. One should read over carefully the Epistle to the Hebrews, an ancient Christian sermon, included in the New Testament, which brings out this priestly role of Christ.

And finally, Christ is King. What does it mean to be King? It means absolute sovereignty, absolute ruler, absolute master. The Kingship of Christ is proclaimed in His resurrection and in the mysterious event which followed it called His ascension to God or into Heaven. Now this is a mystery of mysteries. Most people do not really ponder the greatness of the mystery of Resurrection. It is the first teaching of the Church. Of all of the official dogmatic teachings of the Church, including the Holy Trinity and the Incarnation, the first one to be proclaimed universally and absolutely, the belief that held the Church together in the years of persecution, was that Jesus Christ had risen gloriously from the dead and that the first members of the Church, especially the apostles, were the witnesses to this stupendous event.

Now the Resurrection does not mean merely that the physical body of Jesus Christ was resuscitated, that it came back as did Lazarus or the widow's son. They came back only to die again. That is not the meaning of the Resurrection. Interestingly enough, there are Jewish scholars in the world who believe that Jesus of Nazareth was resuscitated, that His body indeed came back to life and that He spent some time on earth in which time He became the Messiah or the Saviour of the Gentiles. The distinguished Jewish scholar, Pinkas Lapide, is among several Jewish writers who maintain that indeed the body of Jesus Christ was raised. However intriguing and fascinating this teaching is, and however one must admire the intellectual courage of these scholars, nevertheless, this is not the teaching of the Church. The teaching of the Church is that the body of Jesus Christ was reunited with His divine and human nature and that it rose with the life of God; that there was now a particle of matter, a thing of this cosmos, of this created world, which manifests in the most glorious way, its union with the Creator. We believe that there was a human being who was also the Son of God, Who would never die again, Who has gloriously risen from the dead and Who became by reason of this glory our promise of eternal life and of everlasting salvation. This stupendous mystery absolutely affronts those who have no notion of transcendence. If the theory of the scientists on the "big bang" that the cosmos came into existence at a single moment, and if the belief of the Church that Jesus Christ is truly the Son of God causes your mind to reel, here indeed, is something that goes beyond both of these. Both the first and second creation of the world are themselves brought into perspective by the fact that the two worlds, the two domains of being (the transcendent unchangeable domain, that mysterious absolute being we call "God", and the domain of the material cosmos), were so united that there would be forever, without end of end, for ages upon ages, a thing of this material cosmos which participates in the everlasting life of the infinite God. At the Resurrection the cosmos was cracked. There existed in both worlds something of each. Thus the mystery of Divine Love is absolutely manifested in the most tremendous way by the mystery of the Resurrection and Ascension.

For this reason great Christian theologians, as even in modern times, maintained that the mysteries of the Incarnation, Passion and Redemption must always be seen together with the mystery of the Resurrection to make up the one mystery of salvation. Although we were radically saved by the Incarnation, this mystery is not completely seen until we see the glorious Resurrection. And it is for this reason that St. Paul says, "That if Christ is not risen from the dead then our faith is in vain."

The utterly marvelous fact is that this glorious mystery can be summed up in a single life, in fact, in a single name. In the Encyclical, **The Redeemer of Man**, Pope John Paul II sums up the mystery of Christ. "This revelation of the Father and outpouring of the Holy Spirit, which stamp an indelible seal on the mystery of the Redemption, explain the meaning of the cross and death of Christ. The God of creation is revealed as the God of redemption, as the God who is 'faithful to Himself', and faithful to His love for man and the world, which He revealed on the day of creation. His is a love that does not draw back before anything that justice requires in Him. Therefore 'for our sake (God) made him (the Son) to be sin who knew no sin.' If he 'made to be sin' Him who was without any sin whatever, it was to reveal the love that is always greater than the whole of creation, the love that is He Himself, since 'God is Love.' Above all, love is greater than sin, than weakness, than the 'futility of creation', it is stronger than death; it is a love that is

ready to raise up and forgive, always ready to go to meet the prodigal son, always looking for 'the revealing of the sons of God', who are called 'to the glory that is to be revealed'. This revelation of love is also described as mercy, and in man's history this revelation of love and mercy has taken a form and a name; that of Jesus Christ."

The Holy Spirit

We now turn our attention to a topic of greatest importance to many Christians. The meaning and the work of the Holy Spirit. In recent years, the Charismatic Movement, as well as many other encounter movements like the Cursillo, Marriage Encounter, TEC*and many others have focused on the personally felt experience of God which has traditionally been called the work of the Holy Spirit. We are going to look at this today from both its theological and practical point of view, and even make a few suggestions for people who find the work of the Holy Spirit an important part of their life.

Who is the Holy Spirit?

The all-powerful presence of the Holy Spirit is central in both creations. It is in the first creation, in the Book of Genesis, when the Spirit is said to pass over the waters so that they come to life, and in the second creation, that is the Incarnation and Redemption, when in the Gospel of St. Luke the angelic messenger says to Mary, "The Holy Spirit will come upon you and the power of the Most High will cover you with its shadow". Thus in both creations, the Holy Spirit is seen as giving life.

The Jewish people spoke of the Holy Spirit often, but it was Christ who equated this Spirit as a person with the Father and Himself, making the Holy Spirit's

---

*(Teenagers Encounter Christ)

relationship to the Father comparable to His own as Son, and so Christians are baptized according to the command of Christ in the single name of God, the Father, the Son and the Holy Spririt. The ancient theological tradition of the Church sees the Holy Spirit as being the total expression of the love between the Father and the Son. In a word the mystery of God as seen in the New Testament (called the mystery of the Trinity by the Council of Nicea) is a mystery of relationship in which the Holy Spirit is taught as proceeding both from the Father and from the Son. What is perhaps more understandable to most of us is that the Holy Spirit is seen as the source of the constantly extraordinary and powerful works of God in history. The life of the Holy Spirit in the Church is seen to begin at Pentecost, the day when the apostles were filled with the Holy Spirit and went out and did great things, bravely preaching in a mysterious way so that people of different languages were able to understand them. When an unusual conversion occurs or a human being acts beyond his capacity or wounds have been mysteriously healed, both psychological and physical, this is called the work of the Holy Spirit.

St. Paul speaks of the power of the Spirit, of the gifts of the Spirit and of the fruits of the Holy Spirit. These fruits, the effects of the presence of the Holy Spirit on an individual, are quite beautiful. "What the Holy Spirit brings is different, love, joy, peace, patience, kindness, goodness, truthfulness, gentleness and self-control," St. Paul writes in Galatian's V.

He said the Holy Spirit came into the life of the Church. How does it happen that we say that this mysterious presence of God, which gives us power beyond our strength, is indeed the presence of the third person of the Holy Trinity?

The Holy Spirit was sent upon the Church as the climax of Christ's mission and to continue the work of Redemption. Almost among the very last words that Christ speaks to His disciples at the Last Supper are those which pertain to the coming of the Holy Spirit whom Christ promises will help and console them in the dark hours of His passion and in the days ahead. In St. John's Gospel, VI Chapter, as Christ is preparing the apostles for His death, He says, "I did not tell you this from the outset, because I was with you, but now I am going to the one who sent me. Not one of you has asked, where are you going? Yet you are all sad at heart because I have told you this, still I must tell you the truth; it is for your own good that I am going because unless I go, the advocate (the Holy Spirit) will not come to you; but if I do go, I will send him to you. And when he comes, he will show the world how wrong it was, about sin, about who was in the right, and about judgment. . . . I have still many things to say to you, but they would be too much for you now. But when the spirit of truth comes he will lead you to the complete truth, since he will not be speaking as from himself, but he will only be saying what he has learned; and he will tell you of the things to come."

Thus the work of the Holy Spirit is presented by Jesus before His death as a work of reassurance, of teaching, of strengthening and of causing human beings to be able to reach up to the divine.

St. Paul, who was from his own experience of conversion so aware of the power of the Holy Spirit,

teaches us that it is the Spirit who permits us to confess that Jesus is the Lord and it is the Holy Spirit who
cries out within us to God, "Abba, Father". This is an
expression of our belief in God, the Father and the
Son, which comes to us by the inner working of the
Holy Spirit. You might say very logically that without
the Holy Spirit it is impossible to be Christian.

I also want to mention parenthetically that Jewish
mystical writers on the spiritual life have not failed to
give recognition to this unique office of the Holy Spirit
as well. Rabbi Abraham Issac Kook, who was the first
chief Rabbi of Palestine, in his mystical writings tells us
that the music of the Holy Spirit is always sounding in
our souls and that we have only to fall into silence
before God by faith and trust to hear this music of the
Holy Spirit within us. The Rabbi very well points out
that it is not that the Holy Spirit fails to guide us, but
that we fail to listen.

In a century of turmoil and unbelief, of great despair
and great hope among nations, the Church has been
more and more aware of its dependency on the Holy
Spirit. In the last decade, more and more Christians
have experienced in their own lives the healing gifts of
the Holy Spirit, which the Vatican Council taught were
given to all without regard to their rank in the Church.
Although the sacraments confer special charisma or
gifts, such as the priesthood, the gifts of the Holy Spirit
— wisdom, understanding, counsel, knowledge,
courage, fidelity and reverence for the Lord — are
given without regard to rank. They can be given
equally to popes and peddlers, to the powerful and to
the poor. The Holy Spirit becomes the great equalizer

in terms of His gifts. This universality of the gifts of the Holy Spirit is extremely important in a world where countless numbers of individuals need healing and where all of society needs healing. The Jesuit poet Gerard Manley Hopkins, writing at the beginning of our century of the pollution and corruption of the natural and human environment by the industrial revolution, ended his poem with the thought that the dawn of day reminds us that the Holy Spirit constantly broods over the world with bright wings.

Now let me ask you the question, what does the Holy Spirit do in your life? He comes to inspire, to heal, to lead. In relation to the Holy Spirit and His inspiration in our own lives two mistakes can be made. Some are totally deaf to the inspiration of the Holy Spirit in their lives. They don't deny it, but it is something that happens to everybody else, it never happens to them. And so life is bleak and difficult and trying even though they trust in God and try to obey His law. The opposite mistake is made by those who think that all of their thoughts and inclinations are the inspiration of the Holy Spirit. St. John of the Cross used to say that he was terrified by people who went about proclaiming that the Lord had told them this or that, when indeed they were listening to their own imagination. How does one cope with the intrusion of the Holy Spirit into one's life? There are a couple of good rules. One is to be guided by the traditional and deeply spiritual teaching of the Church. Common sense tells us that anyone who has an inspiration had better belong to a community who can correct him or tell him when he is off the deep end. The great theological and traditional structure of the Church is the splendid guide which has led many Christians to great holiness and it is something that causes us to discern and prove the spirits which operate in our life.

A second rule that one might make for the in-telligent use of the inspiration of the Holy Spirit in one's life is to always keep in mind that whatever things we see or learn, be they from our senses, or from internal inspiration, are always deeply colored by our own subjectivity. When you hear the purest message from God it is somewhat warped and fitted to your own ears. This is not because of any weakness of the message but because of how humans perceive things. Peter and Paul both struggled to be guided by the Holy Spirit and they arrived at different answers to the same questions. Those who make the guidance of the Holy Spirit an important part of their lives should carefully keep in mind that when five people read a Bi-ble or a cookbook they all read slightly different things. It can be an intolerable arrogance to impose one's interpretation of the Holy Spirit's inspiration on someone else and be absolutely sure that one is right. I have a little rule of thumb in my life that I use almost every time I meet someone who knows that they are absolutely right. I immediately assume that they must be wrong about something.

I must confess though, that when all is said and done the worst mistakes are made by those who do not let the Holy Spirit enter their lives. They weaken immensely the power of their own life for good. Pope John Paul II in the Encyclical "Redemptor Hominis" has explained that it is one of the great treasures of the Church to teach people to be human in a way that is in keeping with their Christian identity as children of God. There is a creative restlessness, the Pope says, which beats and pulsates deeply in the human heart, a search for truth, for good, a hunger for freedom, a love for the beautiful, a voice of conscience. It is the work of the Christian and the whole Church to keep the human race sensitive to these things. I would like to end our conference today with this quotation on the work of the Holy Spirit.

The words that the Pope ends with are from the sequence of the **Mass of Pentecost** which was written by Archbishop Stephen Langdon, a great leader of the Church, who is also an important person in the history of democracy. It was he who wrote the **Magna Carta**, the document which really began the history of democratic government in the West. The Holy Father writes, "Seeking to see man as it were with the 'eyes of Christ himself,' the Church becomes more and more aware that she is the guardian of a great treasure, which she may not waste but must continually increase. This treasure of humanity enriched by the inexpressible mystery of divine sonship through which we call God, 'Abba, Our Father,' is also the powerful unifying force of the Church above all inwardly and giving meaning to all her activity. Through this powerful force the Church is united with the Spirit of Christ, that the Holy Spirit promised and continually communicated by the Redeemer and whose descent revealed on the day of Pentecost endures forever."

Thus the powers of the Spirit, the gifts of the Spirit, the fruits of the Spirit are revealed in human beings. The present-day Church seems to repeat with greater fervor and with holy insistence, 'Come Holy Spirit,

Come! Come! Heal our wounds, our strength renew;
On our dryness pour your dew; Wash the stains of
guilt away; Bend the stubborn heart and will; Melt the
frozen, warm the chilled; Guide the steps that go
astray.' O most Blessed Light Divine, come within
these hearts of yours, and our inmost being fill.

The Church

We now consider a very simple phrase which may cause all kinds of feelings in our audience — "I believe in the Holy Catholic Church and the Communion of Saints". Many people have mixed emotions about the Church. Some are proud of the Church, others ashamed, some love it, others hate it. Underneath such strong feelings one often finds a trace of the opposite feeling hidden away somewhere. Some people are puzzled by the existence of churches, since they believe in God and do good without belonging to a church. Others are equally puzzled as to how one could live without a church since their place of worship is the center of their lives, not only religiously but socially and in every other way. I hope to present a balanced view of the largest church or religious body in the world, the Catholic Church, as it sees itself from the inside.

My purpose today will not be to launch into a religious argument about the Catholic Church. I used to get into religious arguments in my teens, and I found they were totally useless. Today I want to tell you what the Catholic Church thinks about itself. You may be surprised to learn that what it thinks is somewhat different from what you expected.

The word "church" is a term that means many things. For some people a church is a building, or a collection of buildings scattered around so that they think of the Catholic Church or the Baptist Church merely as a collection of real estate parcels owned by a group of people with similar religious interests · not unlike the collection of people who own fast food franchises. This is really a particularly superficial view of a church which does no justice to any real religious denomination, although it might describe a movement which teaches meditation for specific fees or even the practice of karate.

The word "church" which expresses the same idea as the word "synagogue" means a congregation or a group of people who are called together or assembled to worship God and to support one another in seeking to do His Will and follow His laws. A church or any other religious congregation should not simply be an institution but rather seen as a group of people who are called together with concern for each other and with enthusiasm for a common cause, honoring God and following His laws, including the responsibility of doing good works for others.

In the Acts of the Apostles one finds such a community. One can find them today in small country congregations, or in many religious communities like the religious orders of the Church. But the Church survives when this beautiful ideal of the holy community is not fully realized, because of such factors as the vast number of believers one finds in a great city, or because of religious indifference or a generalized paganism. The Church struggles on without the great personal and emotional support that the ideal of the holy community demands.

This survival of the Church causes us to ask if there is something more to the Church than loyalty and sharing? This is the question that is raised by the survival of the Church in bad times. The answer to this question may provide the answer to why the Catholic Church has survived 2,000 years. The Catholic Church, the Christian community which has operated under the pastoral office of the ordained successors of the apostles, called bishops, and especially the Bishop of Rome (called Pope or Holy Father), has survived through thick and thin. The Catholic Church is so large, so old, and has existed under so many conditions that almost anything you say about it is true. It has given the world saints and sinners of great renown, like the gentle St. Francis and the ominous Inquisitor Torquemada. Absolutely contradictory people will attend its masses on Sunday; a military dictator in Latin America may go to church on Sunday morning and hear himself and his policies denounced from the altar by his bishop. The Church in every age finds room for the oddest contradictions and it is only years afterwards that its saints are recognized. Joan of Arc was burned at the stake as a witch, only to be later canonized a saint; while the bishop who refused to honor her appeal to the pope died excommunicated and disgraced. That is the history of the Catholic Church. It is a study in contrasts. That is part of being Catholic.

Possibly one of the most astonishing contrasts occurred right in Philadelphia in the 19th century. Two men who had been ordained bishops of the Catholic Church died in Philadelphia in the first half of that century. One was the holy and totally dedicated Bishop of Philadelphia, John Neumann, who was canonized a saint only two years ago. The other was Talleyrand,

St. John Neumann

the former French foreign minister and the most excommunicated man in church history, who nevertheless died asking for and receiving the last sacraments of the Church.

All this should not surprise you since the Catholic Church does not see itself as a collection of holy souls. That's the Communion of Saints. Rather the Catholic Church is a collection of poor sinners needing salvation and constantly requiring repentance and mercy from God.

It may surprise you to know that the Catholic Church sees itself as responsible for all the baptized, and in some way for all of mankind. In the decree on the Church, **LUMEN GENTIUM**, the Second Vatican Council declares "All those who in faith look toward Jesus, the Author of salvation and principle of unity and peace, God has gathered together and established as the Church, that it may be for each and every one, the visible sacrament of this saving unity. Destined to extend to all regions of the earth, the Church enters into human history though it transcends at once all times and racial boundaries. Advancing through trials and tribulations, the Church is strengthened by God's grace promised to her by the Lord so that she may not waver from perfect fidelity, but remain the worthy bride of the Lord, until, through the cross, she may attain to that light which knows no setting."

The Catholic Church believes that it, or rather she (because Catholics think of their Church as their mother), survives because she is not only a human organization but she is also the people of God, grown out of Israel, led by Christ, her High Priest, to pursue God and do the works of salvation. The fathers of the Vatican Council give this final summary of the nature of the Church; they declare, "Christ the Lord, high priest taken from among men, made the new people a kingdom of priests to God, His Father. The baptized, by regeneration and anointing of the Holy Spirit, are consecrated to be a spiritual house and a holy priesthood, that through all the works of Christian people they may offer spiritual sacrifices and proclaim the perfection of Him who has called them out of darkness into His marvelous light. Therefore, all the disciples of Christ, persevering in prayer and praising God, should present themselves as a sacrifice, living, holy and pleasing to God. They should everywhere on earth bear witness to Christ and give an answer to everyone who asks a reason for the hope and eternal life which is theirs."

The Catholic Church was given many tools to accomplish this work. These tools include the sacraments, signs by which Christ operates through the Church. It might be well to list them: Baptism, Confirmation, Holy Eucharist, Reconciliation, the Anointing of the Sick, the Ordination of deacons, priests and bishops, and Marriage.

The great sign of the Church which everyone is most familiar with is the Eucharist or the Liturgy, or as it is called popularly, the Mass. It's what the Church sees as its participation on earth in the heavenly offering of Christ as the Son of God, and all the saints with Him, to the Heavenly Father. It is impossible now to tell you all about the Eucharist. It's a presence of

Christ in the world. It is a sacrament which strengthens and nourishes the spiritual life of the individual, and it is a profound sharing in grace. And most importantly it is the re-presentation of the sacrifice which Christ made on Calvary and which was brought to a glorious completion in His Resurrection.

When most people think about the Catholic Church, it is about that Sacrament which they think, and indeed if you have watched events on TV like the installation of a pope, even many non-Catholics have become familiar with the Eucharist. In a great over-simplification, it is easiest to think of this Eucharist as a sharing in the life of the Communion of Saints with Christ in the eternal life. However, the Eucharist also has its important focus in this world in that it is the table to which all mankind are called to share in union with Christ.

When most people think of the Catholic Church, they also think of the pope, the Bishop of Rome. Why Rome and not Jerusalem? Because Christ appointed Peter to take His place after His death as we read in Matthew 16, and Peter died, crucified on the Vatican Hill as the first "bishop" of the Church of Rome. The word "bishop" interestingly enough, literally means "overseer". Since Peter, there have been almost 270 Bishops of Rome and since his death they have in various ways and through many troubles been recognized as chief bishops or head of the church. Most Protestant Christians don't realize the great reformers, especially Luther, did not object to the fact of the Bishop of Rome, but to what in the course of troubled times Rome had become. Recently, an

Episcopal clergyman who is a dear friend of mine was having a discussion with me on a dispute he was having with one of the policies of Pope John Paul II, and he waved his finger at me and said, "Don't forget, Benedict, he is my pope too". Most non-Catholic Christians don't realize that the most important element in their spiritual lives has come to them through the Bishop of Rome, that is the New Testament. It was St. Jerome, a Cardinal of the Catholic Church, who provided Pope Damasus with the first official edition and list of inspired books in the New Testament at the beginning of the Fifth Century. It was on the authority of this pope that the New Testament was accepted.

The Eucharist and the successors of the apostles help us to identify the Church through the ages. As a distinguished Protestant biblical scholar, C. H. Dodd, points out in his book, **The Founder of Christianity**, we can identify the unbroken existence of the Christian community from the time of the Resurrection by the fact that Sunday after Sunday since then the disciples of Christ have gathered to celebrate the Holy Eucharist. This Holy Eucharist is the very center of the life of the Catholic Church. Brother Roger of Taize, the great ecumenical monk, maintains that the Real Presence of Christ in the Eucharist has sustained the Church through thick and thin. The Real Presence of Christ operating in the world is to be found in this most holy sacrament of the Church.

The Church on earth is a very mysterious thing; an odd blend of the human and divine. Its first appointed officials, the apostles, failed miserably in the hour of the passion of Christ and one of the humblest of members, Mary Magdalene (whom Christ had delivered from diabolical influences), was the first witness of the Resurrection — an example of the divine sense of honor.

When you try to evaluate the Catholic Church, or in fact any other religion, I think you should consider its best members. Don't look at its failures. If you want to study and learn from the Jewish religion, take the Prophets, ancient and modern, including such contemporary figures as Rabbi Abraham Isaac Kook and Rabbi Abraham Heschel. If you want to understand the spirit of the Salvation Army, then examine the life of its marvelous founder, General Booth. The Orthodox Church has a whole army of saints ranging from those of long ago like St. Sergius to St. Herman of Alaska who died in our own century. The Lutheran faith in modern times has given us such great Christians as Dietrich Bonhoeffer and Dag Hammarskjold. I could go on and on, through each of the great denominations.

If you look at the Catholic Church look at its saints, the people that the Church itself has chosen as representatives of its ideals. The Catholic Church is not reluctant in telling you who it thinks its saints are. Just here in America they range from the early Jesuit missionaries like St. Isaac Jogues, who was tortured and maimed and escaped to be nursed back to health by the Dutch Calvinists in New Amsterdam only to return and be killed laboring with the Iroquois Indians. The list of American saints includes an Indian girl, Blessed Catherine Tekakwitha who was one of the converts of St. Isaac Jogues, and it ranges to the indomitable Mother Cabrini who, in dozens of countries, opened up homes for poor immigrant people throughout the world. It includes Mother Seton who was raised an Episcopalian and who established the largest system of free Catholic schools in history, following the rule of the man who was literally the first social worker in history, St. Vincent de Paul. We should not leave out of our list the little black saint, Martin de Porres, the son of a slave, whose funeral in Lima, Peru attracted one of the largest assemblages of human beings known to have gathered in the Western Hemisphere up to that time. I could even mention to you that I was once frequently the altar boy of a man who has been proposed for canonization, the gentle friar, Fr. Solanus Casey, who in the humblest way served the Lord and whose prayers were so powerful that 20,000 people attended his funeral in Detroit in 1957.

I am not suggesting that we should make a contest between the heroes of one church or religion and another. That would be silly. But if you want to appreciate the value of a church, look at the people it presents as its best examples. Look at those whom it says the Holy Spirit has come to live in.

The Catholic Church has even gone so far as to choose for you its most exemplary and important member, not a bishop or a pope, but a housewife. The fathers of the Vatican Council, basing themselves very strongly on Sacred Scripture, proclaimed; "Enriched from the first instant of her conception with the splendor of an entirely unique holiness, the Virgin of Nazareth was hailed by the angel with a divine command as 'full of grace' and to the heavenly messenger she replied 'Behold the handmaiden of the Lord, be it

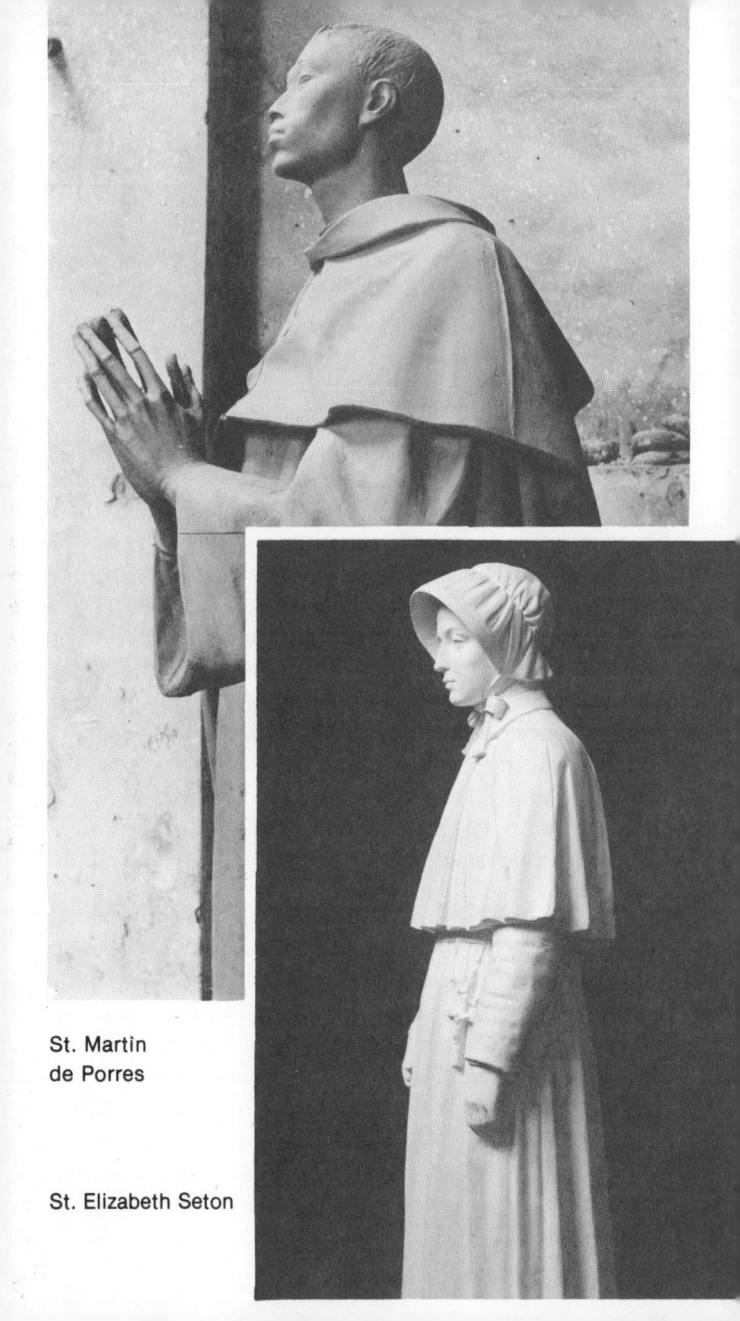

St. Martin
de Porres

St. Elizabeth Seton

done unto to me according to thy word'. Thus the daughter of Adam, Mary, consenting to the word of God becomes Mother of Jesus. Committing herself wholeheartedly and impeded by no sin to God's saving will, she devoted herself totally, as a handmaid of the Lord, to the person and work of her Son, under and with Him, serving the mystery of redemption, by the grace of Almighty God. Rightly, therefore, the fathers see Mary not merely as passively engaged by God, but as freely cooperating in the work of man's salvation through faith and obedience. For as St. Irenaeus says (3rd century) 'She being obedient became the cause of salvation for herself and the whole human race'. The fathers of the Council go on to quote St. Jerome and St. Augustine, two of the most prestigious fathers of the ancient Church, who say respectively, that Mary is the Mother of the living, and that death came through Eve and life through Mary. Therefore, the Vatican Council declared Mary to be the Mother of the Church, the first member of the Church, pre-eminent among the disciples of Christ and one who was entrusted by Christ on the cross to labor for the salvation of mankind.

It is the belief of the vast majority of Christians in the world belonging to the Catholic and Orthodox churches, and even among some Protestants, that Mary continues her work for salvation in eternal life. Everyone knows that it is the duty of a mother to pray for her children. The church has consistently seen Mary as the principal intercessor in union with Christ for the salvation of the world. Pope Paul VI and Pope John Paul II both reiterated that Mary prays in eternal life in a mysterious way for all of those who are called

to salvation. When trying to express this particular belief to an inquiring Jewish friend of mine, I was struggling with the idea that one human being could pray for us all in the mysterious domain of eternal life, in heaven. When I got around to expressing this basic Christian doctrine of the intercession of Mary and the Communion of Saints, stating that those in eternal life could help us on earth by their prayers and concern for us, just as friends on earth pray for each other, I concluded by telling him that Mary prayed for us all since she was the mother of those who were saved through Christ. He looked at me with a twinkle in his eye and he said, "Ah, I see what you are saying; everybody needs to have a Jewish mother".

The Forgiveness of Sin, the Resurrection of the Body and Life Everlasting

Every human being in the world who gives any thought to his or her existence asks constantly: "What will happen to me, and to those dear to me? In fact, what will happen to all mankind? What is the meaning of life? What is the meaning of death? And what will happen after we die?" This is the subject of our last television meditation: "I believe in the forgiveness of sins, the resurrection of the body and life everlasting, Amen." We have seen that the journey of the human race through creation was subject to futility, to meaninglessness, to emptiness. There was no hope. Jesus

Christ came into the world to give human beings a hope in life after death. The Christian religion has offered that promise of Christ to the question of death to billions of people since that first Easter morning. It is a promise not of the simple extension of this life in however pleasant surroundings. Christ has promised that we human beings will share in the life of God, the Heavenly Father. It you wonder about death, your own death, the death of those dear to you, or of all mankind, then join with us for our last meditation.

We began this series with the incredible event, the creation of all the matter in the universe in a single instant. And we saw that the coming of the Son of God into the world, the incarnation of God's own word was an event of even greater magnitude. Today, at the end of our series we pause now for the third mystery of unbelievable magnitude, we ask, what happens after death? What is promised to those who follow the path of salvation when physical life comes to an end? These things are not as remote as you think. A group of scientists recently met in New York and discussed quite calmly the very realistic possibility of the end of the human race by reason of a nuclear war. They pointed out that if all of the nuclear weapons in the world at the present time went off at the same time in some great chain reaction, the entire atmosphere of the planet would be destroyed and the earth would be blown out of its existing orbit. That is a little man-made apocalypse. The death of each one of us is not remote at all. Your television set usually reminds you of people's terrible preoccupation and fear of death.

On television every day there are innumerable make-believe deaths and detective stories and war stories.

And there is an inexhaustible amount of news about real death. People are fascinated by terrible catastrophes and as the natives sometimes do in primitive areas, come with great curiosity to look at the dead. Everyone watching this program is moving toward death at exactly the same rate of speed — 24 hours a day, 7 days a week. Some people watching this program may have reason to think that their death is imminent. They may be what we call "terminally ill". But to be honest, we are all terminally ill with a disease called life. And we are all marching toward death at exactly the same rate of speed. It is important to remember that some of those who have been told that they were dying will get a great deal out of the next few weeks or months of life. And others, who haven't given any thought to death at all, will get nothing out of the next twenty years. This is because some people look at death and face it, and some people run away from it all of their lives, and when it finally catches up with them are plunged into despair.

Today, I would like to present the Christian perspective on death. Everyone knows that the great promise the Christian faith and the Church make to human beings is that they will through faith in Christ be brought through the doors of death into an everlasting life. The promise is given by Christ Himself, by His apostles, especially by St. Paul and in that mysterious book at the very end of the Bible called the Revelation or the Apocalypse. Many people have trouble with this promise because they think it means a simple continuation of this life, a divine life extension institute, as it were. Even though Christ warns us that "eyes have not seen, nor ears heard, nor it has entered into the hearts

rying and scurrying down their road to hell as they tortured innocent human beings to death in the holocaust. As I came around the great tower in the center which was built by the auxiliary bishop of Munich, Dr. Neihauser who had been a prisoner in Dachau for 4½ years, I came to the Carmelite Convent of the Holy Blood. This convent has for its steeple the old gun tower of Dachau Camp. I entered into the chapel whose utterly stark lines are reminiscent of the barracks of the camp and I heard a sound. At first I thought it was the singing of the cloistered nuns who originally come from the Carmelite Convent in Cologne. That was the home of the great Jewish nun, Edith Stein, who died at Auschwitz, both because she was a Jew and because she was a Christian. But no; I realized that this sound I heard was not in my ears but that it was in my soul. It was the singing of a great choir. It was the voices of millions of innocent people who had died in that terrible fire storm of evil which was called the Second World War. Now its victims are at rest.

Perhaps your own thoughts about eternal life are like mine. They often turn to those whom I know and care about and who have died. One of the most consoling doctrines of the Church is that we can pray for the dead and that they can pray for us. Frank Sheed, the great spiritual writer and dear friend of mine, lost his beloved wife a few years ago. I once said to him, "Frank, I am sure you must miss Maizie a lot." This great Christian said to me, "Oh, on the contrary, I feel closer to her than ever before." This is the testimony of faith. There is no way to prove such an experience, it is only possible to have it.

Edith Stein—Sister Benedicta of the Cross

The great Russian writer, Dostoevsky in **Brothers Karamazov**, suggests that we pray every day for someone who will die alone, and that we accompany them as best we can, as an unknown friend, through the doors of death. What a powerful thought! How real it is each day to choose some unknown person who will die alone and to accompany them to the throne of God.

We began this series with the explosion of creation. We carried it through to the explosion of Divine Love, which took place in the birth, life, death and resurrection of Jesus Christ, Our Lord, the love of God communicated to the world. And now we see it end, in another great explosion. This explosion, like the first and second, is both an end of something and the beginning of something else. It is the beginning of everlasting life. The last book of the Bible gives us the description of this event in symbols. It is this for which the believer waits. It is even this which the skeptic and the unbeliever must hope to be true. There is no human being who could die, who in the depths of his heart when he thought about it, would not wish that the promise of the last book of Sacred Scripture might be true. In the Book of Revelation we read: "And then I saw a new heaven and a new earth. The first heaven and the first earth had disappeared now, and there was no longer any sea. I saw the Holy City, and the new Jerusalem, coming down from God out of heaven, as beautiful as a bride all dressed for her husband. Then I heard a loud voice call from the throne, 'You see this city? Here God lives among men. He will make his home among them; they shall be His people, and He will be their God; His name is God-with-them.

He will wipe away all tears from their eyes, there will be no death, no mourning or sadness. The world of the past has gone.' "

With these stirring words, we end our simple meditations on the Creed. May I suggest to you that you get to know your faith better; that you pray with it and pray in it, that you live with it. Faith makes it possible to go on with hope and love. And if you do not have faith, pray also. Pray, even if you don't believe; and faith will be given to you.

Talks of John Paul II

With Foreword by His Eminence, John Cardinal Krol

109 addresses, from October 16, 1978, to the end of December. The addresses are presented in their entirety. 17 four-color photographs; 35 black and white photographs. 542 pages
cloth $7.95; paper $6.95 — RA0188

"You Are the Future, You Are My Hope"

Pope John Paul II
Compiled and indexed by the Daughters of St. Paul

Volume one of talks of His Holiness *to young people* of all ages. Reveals the stirring personal appeal of the Pope to the new generation. Excellent for youth and those involved in guidance. 326 pages; 16 pages of full-color photos
cloth $4.95; paper $3.95 — EP1120

I Believe in Youth, Christ Believes in Youth

Pope John Paul II
Compiled and indexed by the Daughters of St. Paul

A second volume of the Pope's talks to youth. 304 pages
cloth $4.95; paper $3.95 — EP0586

The Catechism of Modern Man

Edited and compiled by a team of Daughters of St. Paul
Best Seller

—Over 9,000 topics—**The Catechism of Modern Man** is the only complete source of the Council's new and profound expression of the Faith—all in the words of Vatican II and related post-conciliar documents. 731 pages; plastic or cloth $7.95; paper $6.95 — RA0020

Living the Catholic Faith Today

Most Rev. John F. Whealon, STD, SSL, DD

This short volume packs a wealth of insights on practicing the Catholic faith now. Among many topics—Why believe in God; Why be a Roman Catholic; Ideas on parish life; Practial Ideas on Confession; How should a Catholic live the faith. A book to be owned by every Catholic adult and inquirer into the faith.
130 pages
cloth $2.50; paper $1.50 — RA0130

Basic Catechism

Daughters of St. Paul

This concise, direct book presents the fundamentals of the Catholic Faith in a question-and-answer format with related scriptural quotations.

Thoroughly indexed for ready reference, it is a vital handbook for anyone desiring to deepen or clarify his belief. 208 pages
cloth $3.00; paper $1.50 — RA0007

The Faith We Live By

Daughters of St. Paul

One of the magnificent legacies left us by Pope Paul—his Credo of the People of God, entirely explained in these pages. A tremendous background source on the Catholic faith steeped in Scripture, quotations from the Fathers of the Church and Vatican II documents—poems, prayers, photos! 400 pages
cloth $7.00; paper $6.00 — CA0110

The Catholic Church Through the Ages

Rev. Martin P. Harney, SJ

Thorough and factual. The author, historian and long-time Church history professor, treats every major issue from the era of primitive Christianity up into our own twentieth century. His style reveals his familiarity with the events he relates. Ideal as reference material, this newest work could also lend itself very well to classroom use. 600 pages
cloth $12.00; paper $11.00 — RA0030

Order from addresses on the following page. Please specify title and item number.

Daughters of St. Paul

IN MASSACHUSETTS
   50 St. Paul's Ave., Jamaica Plain, Boston, MA 02130;
      617-522-8911; 617-522-0875
   172 Tremont Street, Boston, MA 02111; **617-426-5464;**
      617-426-4230
IN NEW YORK
   78 Fort Place, Staten Island, NY 10301; **212-447-5071**
   59 East 43rd Street, New York, NY 10017; **212-986-7580**
   7 State Street, New York, NY 10004; **212-447-5071**
   625 East 187th Street, Bronx, NY 10458; **212-584-0440**
   525 Main Street, Buffalo, NY 14203; **716-847-6044**
IN NEW JERSEY
   Hudson Mall — Route 440 and Communipaw Ave.,
      Jersey City, NJ 07304; **201-433-7740**
IN CONNECTICUT
   202 Fairfield Ave., Bridgeport, CT 06604; **203-335-9913**
IN OHIO
   2105 Ontario St. (at Prospect Ave.), Cleveland, OH 44115; **216-621-9427**
   25 E. Eighth Street, Cincinnati, OH 45202; **513-721-4838**
IN PENNSYLVANIA
   1719 Chestnut Street, Philadelphia, PA 19103; **215-568-2638**
IN VIRGINIA
   1025 King St., Alexandria, VA 22314
IN FLORIDA
   2700 Biscayne Blvd., Miami, FL 33137; **305-573-1618**
IN LOUISIANA
   4403 Veterans Memorial Blvd., Metairie, LA 70002; **504-887-7631;**
      504-887-0113
   1800 South Acadian Thruway, P.O. Box 2028, Baton Rouge, LA 70821
      504-343-4057; 504-343-3814
IN MISSOURI
   1001 Pine Street (at North 10th), St. Louis, MO 63101; **314-621-0346;**
      314-231-1034
IN ILLINOIS
   172 North Michigan Ave., Chicago, IL 60601; **312-346-4228**
      312-346-3240
IN TEXAS
   114 Main Plaza, San Antonio, TX 78205; **512-224-8101**
IN CALIFORNIA
   1570 Fifth Avenue, San Diego, CA 92101; **714-232-1442**
   46 Geary Street, San Francisco, CA 94108; **415-781-5180**
IN HAWAII
   1143 Bishop Street, Honolulu, HI 96813; **808-521-2731**
IN ALASKA
   750 West 5th Avenue, Anchorage AK 99501; **907-272-8183**
IN CANADA
   3022 Dufferin Street, Toronto 395, Ontario, Canada
IN ENGLAND
   128, Notting Hill Gate, London W11 3QG, England
   133 Corporation Street, Birmingham B4 6PH, England
   5A-7 Royal Exchange Square, Glasgow G1 3AH, England
   82 Bold Street, Liverpool L1 4HR, England
IN AUSTRALIA
   58 Abbotsford Rd., Homebush, N.S.W., Sydney 2140, Australia